Jeff Zimmerman
presented by
R 20th Century Gallery and Gallery Seomi

GALLERY
SEOMI

whitehaus

Jeff Zimmerman
Edited by Zesty Meyers and Cate Andrews
Essay by Rachel Wolff
Photographs by Sherry Griffin (pages 58-59, 64, 65, 67 by Myoungrae Park for Gallery Seomi)
Art Direction by Carlos Suarez
Editorial Direction by Sarah Harrelson and Tali Jaffe
Produced by R 20th Century Gallery in collaboration with Seomi Gallery and Whitehaus Media

R 20th Century Gallery
82 Franklin Street
New York, NY 10013
T: 212 343 7979 F: 212 343 0226
www.r20thcentury.com

ISBN-13: 978-0-9704608-5-1

Distribution in North America by
ARTBOOK | D.A.P.
155 Sixth Avenue, 2nd Floor
New York, NY 10013
www.artbook.com

Printed and bound by
Shapco Printing, Inc.
524 North Fifth Street
Minneapolis, MN 55401
www.shapco.com

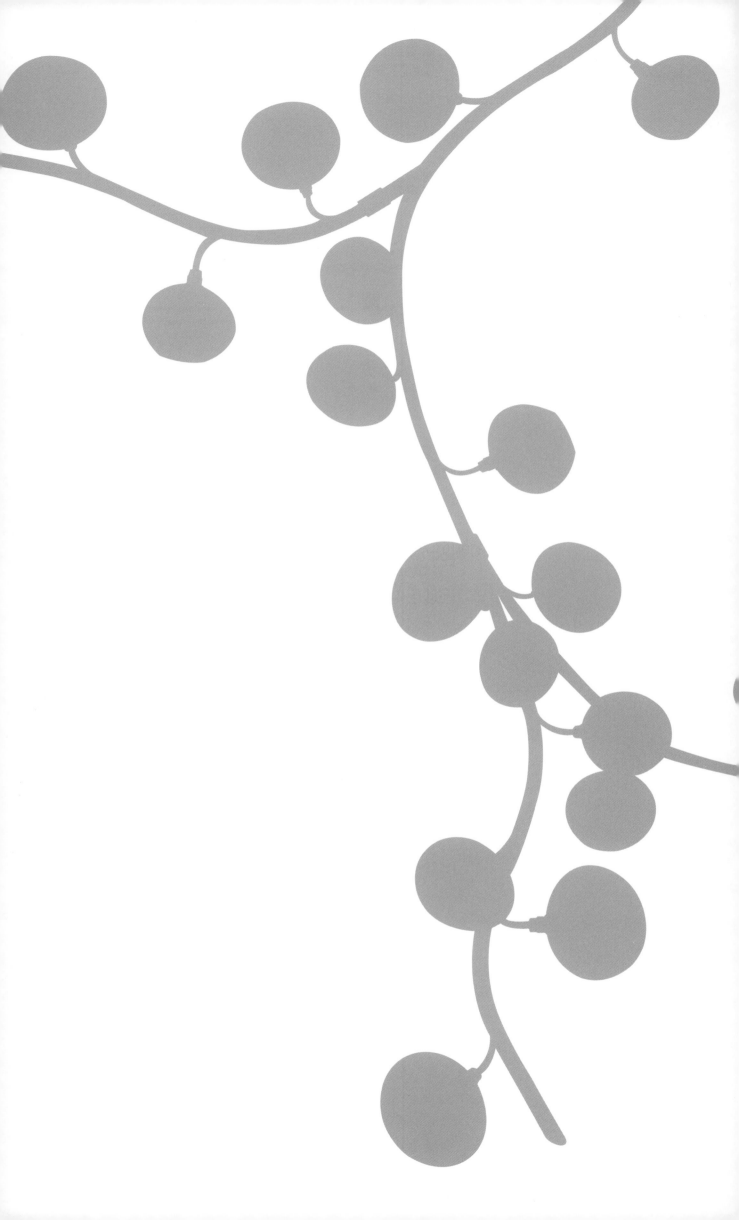

JEFF ZIMMERMAN

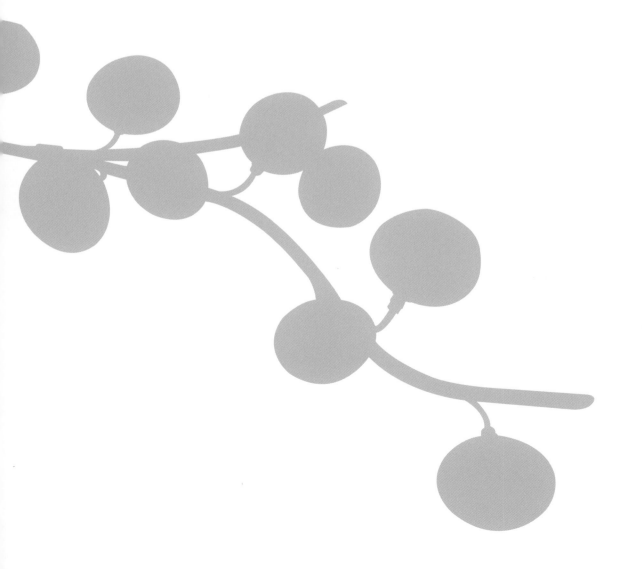

FOREWORD

This catalogue illustrates how Jeff Zimmerman's artistic ideas and virtuosic abilities have evolved and deepened over many years. With this new collection, he creates a visual concert of spectacular forms that play off one another beautifully.

The works are derived from natural forms and inspired by the imagery of molecular architecture, the layering of feathers and the innate temporality of a soap bubble or the bud of a flower. Zimmerman also uses techniques such as mirrorizing to play with the perception of reality and the hypnotic distortions of a reflective surface.

There is inherent warmth, a seduction even, that sets Zimmerman's work apart. His forms are timelessly elegant, and sometimes so minimal that they belie the extraordinary technical skill it actually takes to make them. Zimmerman's hand—and his incomparable vision—directs every facet of the process, from drawing to model to finished form. Each piece is alive with the authenticity and intimacy of the handmade.

Many of his pieces are site-specific commissions. Among Zimmerman's many gifts, one that stands out to me is his unique ability to design a piece that resonates in absolute harmony with the art and architecture cohabiting a space, and with the individuals who live there.

—*Zesty Meyers, R 20th Century Gallery*

Like an instantaneously paused stage, Jeff Zimmerman's works are views into a momentary scene. Together, glass orbs form an elegant banquet of light that implies a poem or epic narrative, reminiscent of constellations, organic forms of nature, a symphony, movement of dancers, or particles in space.

Zimmerman's works are of both bold and delicate sensibilities, containing time and process of an erratic amorphous medium becoming an attractive and warm object of light through natural and physical conditions like fire, air and water. Their dynamism emits delicate light and flows through still tranquility, provoking curiosity and awe that brings life into a space. Glass orbs carry their own breath and movement as inanimate objects, and are fascinating in that they become symbols of frozen narratives.

His works are spectacular and simplified expressions of illusion or fantasy of some sort, realized into objects. The original ideas and artisan spirit, and delicate sensitivity toward the medium is, in his collection, fused into a synesthetic aesthetic. Zimmerman upends traditional methods of glass art and his creations take a fundamental approach in the medium and challenge it toward a new scope, uniting a space and its inhabitants with light and embracing various spectrums in culture.

—*P.J. Park, Gallery Seomi*

Zimmerman designing in his studio, New York, 2009.

Jeff Zimmerman's elegant, singular and genre-defying glasswork begs to be touched. Zimmerman so adeptly creates the dents, the crumples, the textures and the curves that in order to get a sense of the objects' fragility, their weight and their texture, one is physically drawn to reach out and feel them.

Zimmerman can often be found hard at work in a glass-blowing studio in Red Hook, a remote industrial corner of Brooklyn overlooking the New York harbor. He and his two assistants are scarily in sync, working in near silence with the sort of choreographed ease that comes only at this level of skill. Zimmerman is undoubtedly the one in control, overseeing every step of the process. He gives the occasional instruction—more heat, more breath, more glass—and is often the one at the reins, wielding the steel rod to which this blistering molten goo is affixed as if it were a fifth limb.

His tools are basic. Aside from the glass itself (maintaining its liquid form in a 2000° oven), there's fire (to heat), air and water (to cool), gravity, strength, measured momentum, and a series of lo-fi accessories made out of cherry wood, cork, newspaper,

and steel (think paddles, pads, tweezers, shears, and glass-wielding rods). The lava-like medium is gathered on the poles then rolled, blown, flamed, and tempered until perfect spheres take shape. Then, just as deftly and deliberately, Zimmerman completely messes them up, whipping, pressing, and pulling the glass into shapes that don't seem remotely possible like crumpled orbs, tentacled urchins, and elongated tears. It's a way of working that distinguishes Zimmerman from others in his field and a brand of innovation that is akin to the ways in which artists like Pablo Picasso and Alexander Calder upended their classical training to make something different and new.

When he's not blowing glass in Red Hook, Zimmerman works out of a small studio in Williamsburg, another artistic enclave in Brooklyn. It's a more meditative space that, in its fabulous clutter, shows the many currents of Zimmerman's active mind. He equates much of what he does to drawing, working with the architecture of a wall or a space as a draftsman might approach the confines and possibilities of a blank page. It's a mantra that extends to his installations and his lighting commissions,

Zimmerman blowing glass, New York, 2011.

as well as the dozens of artworks scattered throughout his studio that he's made just for fun (a personal favorite: a snow-covered cliff crafted from picked-apart Styrofoam and dotted with miniature figurines).

It's here in Williamsburg that Zimmerman's "drawings" come to life. He lays out the components (some of which have been tinted or mirrorized at this point to enhance their effects) on the floor and moves them around until they make sense. Single misshapen teardrops are arranged into large nebulous splashes that will later be mounted on gallery walls. Mini spheres are clustered together, not unlike the minute particles from which they are comprised, to form floor sculptures and globular chandeliers. And dented ellipses are lined up into compositions that could be read as anything from a wailing and abstracted Greek chorus to a craggy and rain-slicked swath of land. Other glass pieces are integrated into Zimmerman's one-off light fixtures, which as of late have taken the form of serpentine brass vines studded with dented globes.

There is an indelible connection between Zimmerman's virtuosic handling of glass and what he uses it to communicate.

Zimmerman shaping glass, New York, 2011.

ZIMMERMAN IS OFTEN THE ONE AT
THE REINS, WIELDING THE STEEL ROD
TO WHICH BLISTERING MOLTEN GOO
IS AFFIXED AS IF IT WERE A FIFTH LIMB.

Many parallels have been drawn between the shapes of his work and those found in nature, but Zimmerman's connections to the natural world go far deeper than aesthetic similarities. When he speaks about his work, he makes reference to quantum physics, metaphysics, and the phenomenon of freezing time. He has an utter fascination with the perfect, flawed, and hypnotic patterns that occur on every scale, from the infinitesimal on up. And he is far less interested in the way things look than he is in the mystical reactions, eruptions, and happy accidents that bore them in the first place. It's this that he seeks to emulate and it's this that he uses glass—a fittingly difficult, unforgiving, and precarious medium—to question and express.

Even after all this time, it's clear that Zimmerman is still completely seduced by the magic of his medium. Though beautiful and significant all on their own, Zimmerman's objects are also relics—"frozen narratives," as he puts it, documenting quiet and hypnotic performances in which glass is forced far above and beyond its historical potential—and performances that a few of us have been lucky enough to see.—*Rachel Wolff*

Zimmerman reheating glass in the "glory hole," New York, 2011.

VINES

Vine illuminated sculpture, detail, 2011.

Vine illuminated sculpture, detail, 2011.

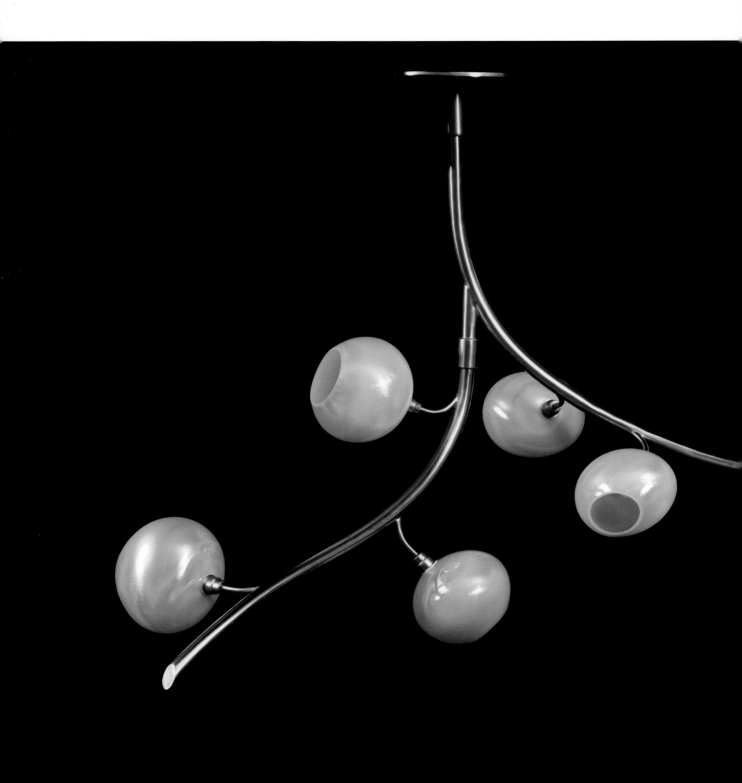

Vine illuminated sculpture, 2007.

Vine illuminated sculpture, detail, 2011.

MANY PARALLELS HAVE BEEN DRAWN BETWEEN THE SHAPES OF HIS WORK AND THOSE FOUND IN NATURE, BUT HIS CONNECTIONS TO THE NATURAL WORLD GO FAR DEEPER THAN AESTHETIC SIMILARITIES.

Vine illuminated sculpture drawing, 2009.

Vine illuminated sculpture, 2011.

Vine illuminated sculpture, 2011.

Vine illuminated sculpture installation at R 20th Century, New York, 2011.

Vine illuminated sculpture, detail, 2011.

Vine illuminated sculpture drawing, 2011.

Vine illuminated sculpture, detail, 2011.

Vine illuminated sculpture, detail, 2011.

SILVER

Silver Dented sculptures in mirrorized glass, 2011.

DENTED ELLIPSES ARE LINED UP INTO
COMPOSITIONS THAT COULD BE READ
AS ANYTHING FROM A WAILING AND
ABSTRACTED GREEK CHORUS TO A CRAGGY
AND RAIN-SLICKED SWATH OF LAND.

Silver Dented sculptures in mirrorized glass, 2011.

Silver Dented sculptures in mirrorized glass, 2011.

Silver Dented sculpture in mirrorized glass, detail, 2011.

Silver Dented sculptures in mirrorized glass, 2011.

Silver Cube sculptures in mirrorized glass, 2011.

Silver Asteroid sculptures in mirrorized glass, 2010.

Silver Asteroid sculptures in mirrorized glass, detail, 2010.

Silver sculptures in mirrorized glass, 2011.

THOUGH BEAUTIFUL AND SIGNIFICANT ALL ON THEIR OWN, ZIMMERMAN'S OBJECTS ARE ALSO RELICS, "FROZEN NARRATIVES," AS HE PUTS IT, DOCUMENTING THE QUIET AND HYPNOTIC PERFORMANCES IN WHICH GLASS IS FORCED FAR ABOVE AND BEYOND ITS HISTORICAL POTENTIAL.

Silver sculptures in mirrorized glass, 2011.Silver sculptures in mirrorized glass, 2011.

Silver Opalescent Splash sculptures in mirrorized glass, 2011.

IT'S IN ZIMMERMAN'S STUDIO THAT HIS "DRAWINGS" COME TO LIFE... HE LAYS OUT THE COMPONENTS ON THE FLOOR AND MOVES THEM AROUND UNTIL THEY MAKE SENSE.

Silver Opalescent Splash sculptures in mirrorized glass, 2011.

Splash sculptures drawing, 2010.

Silver Opalescent Splash sculptures in mirrorized glass, 2011.

Silver Splash sculptures in mirrorized glass, 2011.

Silver Splash sculptures in mirrorized glass, 2011.

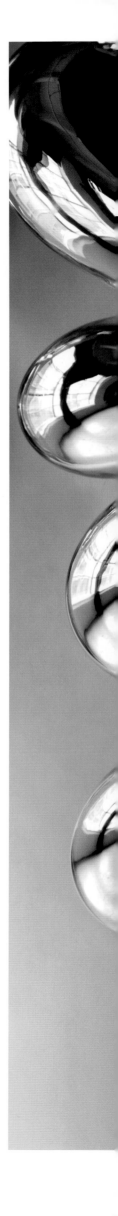

Silver Splash sculptures in mirrorized glass, 2011.

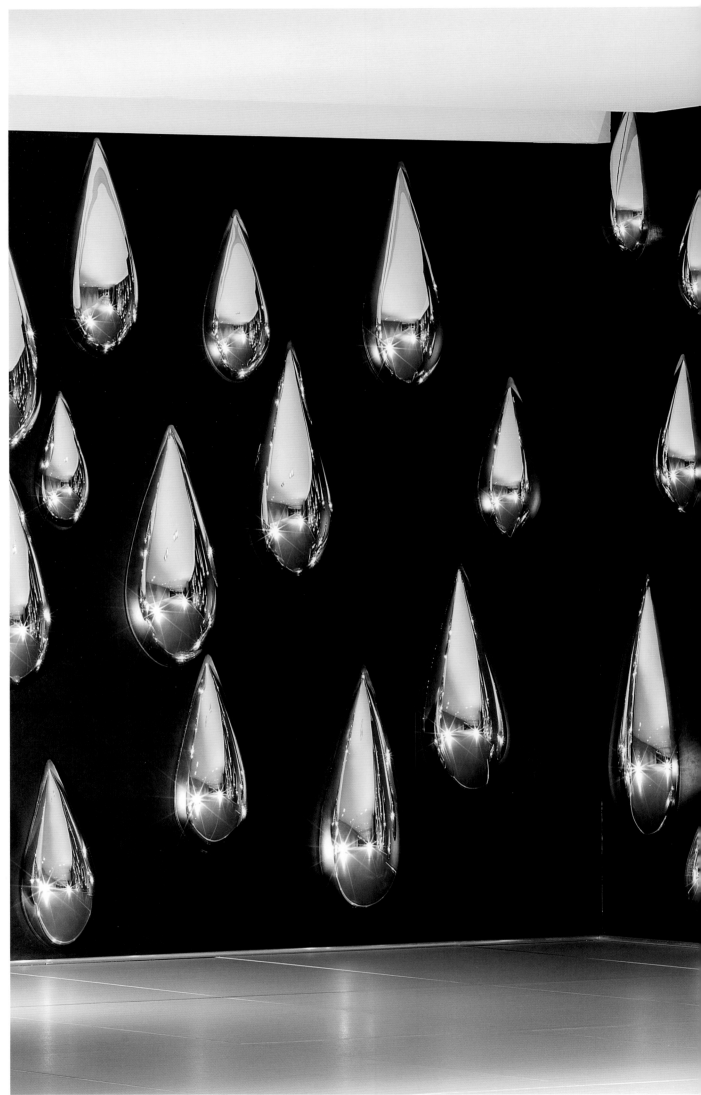

Silver Surfer Tears sculptures installation at Hyundai Capital, Seoul, Korea, 2011.

Silver Surfer Tears sculptures in mirrorized glass, 2010.

Silver Surfer Tears sculptures installation in Zimmerman's exhibition *Drawings in Glass*, R 20th Century, New York, 2009.

CLUSTERS

Bubble Cluster illuminated sculpture installation at Hyundai Capital, Seoul, Korea, 2011.

Bubble Cluster illuminated sculpture installation at Hyundai Capital, Seoul, Korea, 2011.

HE HAS AN UTTER FASCINATION WITH THE PERFECT, FLAWED AND HYPNOTIC PATTERNS THAT OCCUR ON EVERY SCALE, FROM THE INFINITESIMAL ON UP.

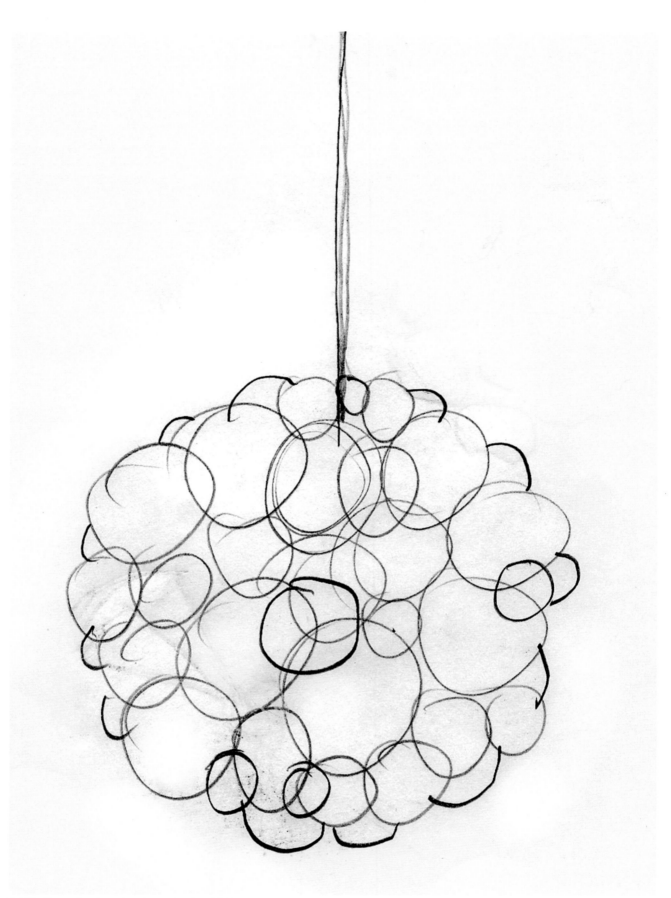

Bubble Cluster illuminated sculpture drawing, 2010.

Bubble Cluster illuminated sculpture, detail, 2011.

Bubble Cluster illuminated sculpture, 2008.

Bubble Cluster illuminated sculpture, 2008.

Bubble Cluster illuminated sculpture, detail, 2008.

Bubble Cluster illuminated sculptures drawings, 2010.

Feather Cluster illuminated sculpture installation in Zimmerman's exhibition *Drawings in Glass*, R 20th Century, New York, 2009.

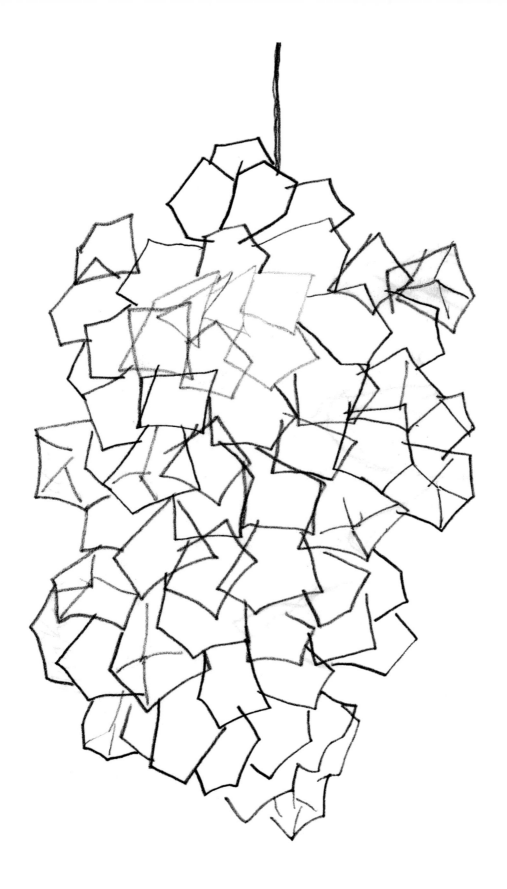

Cluster illuminated sculpture drawing, 2010.

Feather Cluster illuminated sculpture, 2008.

Feather Cluster illuminated sculpture, 2008.

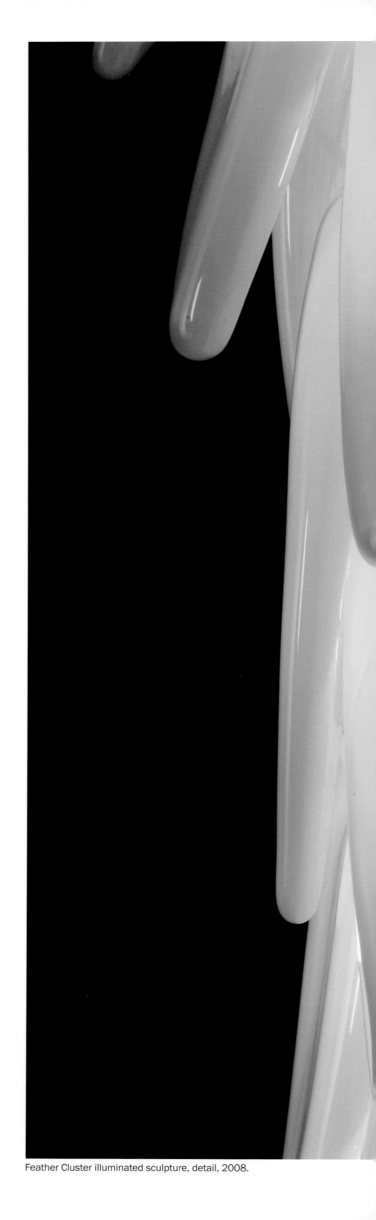

Feather Cluster illuminated sculpture, detail, 2008.

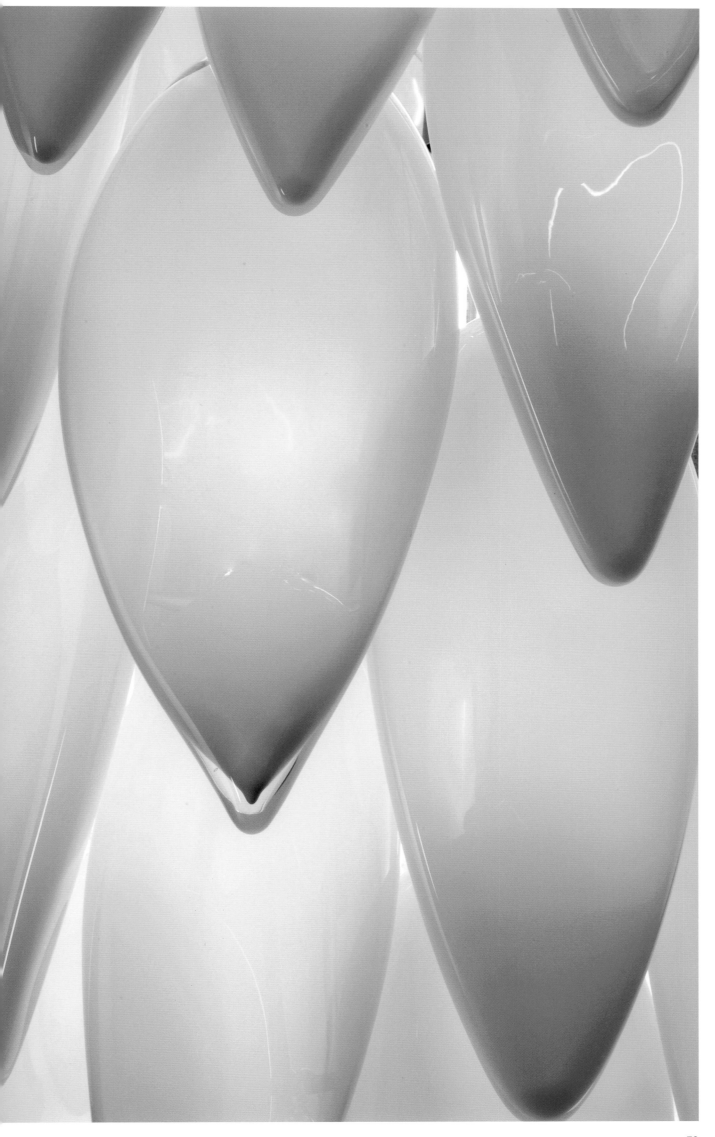

ACKNOWLEDGMENTS

This catalogue, and the work represented herein, would not have been possible without the incredible efforts of our entire staff here at R 20th Century, including Frances Perkins, Jill McKenna, Lily Kane, Veralyn Behenna and Tristan Fitch. We would especially like to thank staff members Sherry Griffin, for her incredible photography; Jude Hughes and John Stendrini for helping engineer the mechanics of installation and illumination; and Cate Andrews for production coordination at every level.

We are grateful to P.J. Park at Gallery Seomi for collaborating on this publication. Carlos Suarez, Sarah Harrelson and Tali Jaffe at Whitehaus Media, whom we were thrilled to work with, as always. We thank Rachel Wolff for her insightful text.

Most importantly, we thank Jeff Zimmerman for continuing to make work that truly inspires us.

—*Zesty Meyers and Evan Snyderman, R 20th Century Gallery*

TRANSLATION

FOREWORD

이 도록은 제프 짐머만(Jeff Zimmerman)의 예술적 사고와 장인적인 능력의 변화와 발전된 모습을 보여주고 있다. 그는 이 새로운 작품들을 통해, 극적인 형체들이 아름답게 조화되는 시각적 화음을 만들어내고 있다.

그의 작품들은 자연의 모습에 기초하여 분자의 구성, 깃털의 중첩된 형태, 비누방울의 일시성 또는 꽃봉오리에 영감을 받아 만들어졌으며, 거울화 기법을 사용해 반사면이 보여주는 현실에 대한 자각이나 최면을 거는 듯한 왜곡을 재미있게 담아내고 있다.

짐머만의 작품들은 특유의 따뜻함에 유혹적인 매력까지 더해져 차별화된다. 그가 만들어내는 사물들은 불멸의 우아함을 지니며, 때로는 매우 단순한 형상을 나타내기도 하는데, 창작에 있어 실제로 요구되는 뛰어난 기법은 쉽게 드러나지 않는다. 작가는 남다른 재능과 시각으로 드로잉에서부터 모형 제작, 완성까지에 이르는 모든 작업 과정을 연출한다. 이러한 과정을 통해, 각각의 작품에는 수작업이 주는 진정성과 친밀감이 숨쉬고 있다.

그의 작품 대부분은 특정 장소에 설치하기 위해 제작된다. 짐머만이 지닌 수 많은 재능 가운데서도 돋보이는 점은, 사람이 생활하는 공간 안에 건축과 예술이 완벽한 조화를 이루는 작품을 디자인하는 그 만의 독창적인 재능이다.

—제스티 마이어스 (Zesty Meyers)

제프 짐머만(Jeff Zimmerman)의 작품들은 마치 순간적으로 정지한 무대를 관람하듯, 찰나의 장면을 바라보는 것과 같다. 유리 구체들이 어우러져 만드는 우아한 빛의 향연은 한 편의 시(詩)나 서사적인 이야기를 함축하고 있으며, 별의 무리, 유기적인 형태의 자연물, 교향곡의 한 악장과 무용수들의 움직임, 우주의 미립자 등을 연상시킨다.

대범하고 섬세한 감성이 동시에 살아있는 짐머만의 작품에는, 불규칙한 성질을 지닌 무정형의 물질이 불과 공기, 물이라는 자연적이고 물리적인 조건을 만나면서 따뜻하고 매력적인 빛의 오브제로 변화하는 과정과 시간이 담겨 있다. 정적인 고요함으로 은은한 빛을 내는 가운데 흐르는 역동성은 호기심과 경외심을 불러일으키며 공간에 생동감을 불어넣는다. 무생물로서의 유리 구체들은 나름대로의 호흡과 움직임을 가지고 있으며, "얼어붙은 이야기"로 상징화 된다는 점에서 매우 흥미롭다.

그의 작품은 일종의 환영이나 환상을 화려하고 단순하게 표현한 현실화된 오브제들이라 할 수 있다. 그의 작업 세계에 존재하는 독창적인 아이디어와 견고한 장인정신은 소재에 대한 섬세한 감성과 결합되어 공감각적 미학을 보여주고 있다. 유리 공예의 전통적인 방식을 뛰어넘어 소재에 대한 본질적인 접근을 통해 만들어진 그의 작품들은 인간과 공간을 빛으로 아우르며 다양한 문화의 스펙트럼을 포용하고 있다.

—박필재, 갤러리서미 이사 (P.J. Park)

ESSAY

제프 짐머만(Jeff Zimmerman)의 작업실은 뉴욕 항구가 내려다 보이는 브루클린(Brooklyn)의 공업지역 레드훅(Red Hook)의 한 외진 곳에 위치하고 있다. 그곳에서 두 명의 조수와 함께 완벽한 호흡으로 침묵 속에 유리 불기(glass blowing) 작업을 하는 짐머만을 만날 수 있다. 그가 모든 작업 단계를 감독하는 가운데, 숙련된 기술자들은 편안하게 호흡을 맞춰 작업에 임한다. 그는 한시도 놓치지 않고 열, 호흡, 유리의 양에 대해 작업 지시를 하면서, 시뻘겋게 달아오른 유리 덩어리가 붙어있는 강철 막대를 마치 몸의 일부인 것처럼 자연스럽게 다루고 있다.

짐머만의 작업도구들은 섭씨 약 2000도의 가마에서 액체상태를 유지하는 유리를 제외하고는 간단하다. 유리를 달구는 불, 그것의 열을 식히기 위한 공기와 물, 중력과 힘을 이용하여 작업의 가속과 탄력을 조절하고, 벚나무, 코르크, 신문지, 등으로 만든 부품들과 강철로 만들어진 기구(주걱, 받침대, 족집게, 절단기, 봉)와 같이 쉽게 볼 수 있는 도구들을 사용한다. 마치 용암과도 같은 유리 덩어리를 가느다란 봉 끝에 모아 완전한 구(球)의 모양이 되기까지 굴리고, 불고, 달구고 담금질하는 과정을 거친다. 그런 다음 작가는 다시 의도적으로 그것들을 망가뜨리는데, 유리 구(球)를 휘젓고, 누르고, 당기어 찌그러진 공, 촉수가 무수한 성게 혹은 늘어진 눈물과도 같은 형상들로 변형 시킨다. 이와 같은 짐머만의 작업방식은 다른 유리 공예 작가들과 확연히 차별되는 것이며, 기존의 개념을 뒤집어 새로운 미학을 제시했던 파블로 피카소(Pablo Picasso), 알렉산더 칼더(Alexander Calder)와 같은 혁신을 떠올리게 한다.

레드훅 스튜디오에서 유리 불기 작업이 없을 때, 짐머만이 작업하는 곳은 브루클린의 또 다른 예술가 밀집 지역인 윌리엄스버그(Williamsburg)이다. 이 공간은 작가가 작업 구상을 하는 곳으로서, 멋지고 다양한 작품들이 모여있는 이 공간에서 활발하게 진행되는 작가의 작업 세계를 엿볼 수 있다. 그는 아이디어의 대부분을 스케치로 완성하는데, 작업실의 벽이나 공간 등 종이의 제한된 화폭을 뛰어넘어 생각을 표현해낸다. 이 공간에는 그의 설치작업들, 컬렉터로부터 주문 받은 조명들, 특히 스티로폼과 작은 오브제들을 이용하여 작가가 재미 삼아 만든 눈 덮인 절벽 등이 어우러져 일종의 만트라를 이루고 있다.

짐머만의 드로잉들은 비로소 윌리엄스버그의 작업실에서 탄생된다. 그는 여러 가지 재료들 -시각적인 효과를 높이기 위해 재료에 색을 칠하거나 거울처럼 만들기도 한다. - 을 바닥에 펼쳐 놓고, 이리저리 움직여가며 형태를 완성한다. 기이한 모양의 눈물 방울들이 모여 성운을 이루어 후에 갤러리 벽에 설치되고, 작은 구(球)체들이 무리를 지어 조형물이 되거나 샹들리에가 되기도 한다. 찌그러진 유리 타원체들의 구성과 조합은 때로는 그리스의 합창 소리, 또는 비바람으로 인해 울퉁불퉁해 진 땅 덩어리를 추상적으로 연상시키기도 하며, 포도나무 넝쿨을 연상시키는 조명으로 만들어진다.

짐머만은 단지 유리를 다루는 장인적인 기법에만 머무르지 않고 작품을 통해 소통하려는 강한 철학을 갖고 있다. 그의 작품들이 지닌 형태가 종종 자연의 형상에 비유되기도 하지만, 그것들이 지닌 자연과의 관계에는 미적, 형태적 유사성 보다 더 깊은 의미가 내재되어 있다.

그가 양자물리학과 형이상학, 그리고 정지된 시간의 현상 등을 언급하며, 무한소에서 우주까지의 모든 규모에서 일어나는 완벽하거나 혹은 부족하기도 한 황홀한 패턴에 매료되어 있다고 설명한다. 유리라는 불안정하고 다루기 어려운 매체를 통하여 외적인 형상 보다는, 그 자체가 가진 초자연적인 반응과 그것을 통한 발생, 그리고 멋진 우연성 들을 탐구하고 표현하고자 하는 것이다.

오랜 시간 동안 유리를 소재로 다양한 작업을 해오면서도, 그는 여전히 그 소재의 무한한 매력에 완전히 매료되어 있다. 짐머만의 작품은 그 자체로도 아름답고 중요한 오브제이면서, 그가 "얼어붙은 이야기"라고 표현하듯, 조용하고 최면적인 행위의 기록이다. 또한, 유리가 지닌 역사적인 가능성을 뛰어넘으며 소수만이 경험할 수 있는 특별한 장면을 기록한 살아있는 유물이기도 한 것이다.

—*Rachel Wolff*

A Book

There is no frigate like a book
To take us lands away,
Nor any coursers like a page
Of prancing poetry.
This traverse may the poorest take
Without oppress of toll;
How frugal is the chariot
That bears a human soul!

Emily Dickinson